GRAPHIC MY

GREEK
MYTHS

by Rob Shone

BOOK HOUSE

Designed and produced by
David West Children's Books
7 Princeton Court
55 Felsham Road
London SW15 1AZ

Editor: Kate Newport

Photo credits:
Page 4 top, Andy Didya/iStockphoto.com

First published in 2006 by **Book House,**
an imprint of The Salariya **Book Company Ltd**
25 Marlborough Place, Brighton BN1 1UB

Please visit the Salariya Book Company at:
www.salariya.com

HB ISBN 1 905087 73 X
PB ISBN 1 905087 74 8

Visit our website at **www.book-house.co.uk**
for free electronic versions of:
You Wouldn't Want to Be an Egyptian Mummy!
You Wouldn't Want to Be a Roman Gladiator!
Avoid joining Shackleton's Polar Expedition!

A catalogue record for this book is available from the British Library.

Printed on paper from sustainable forests.

Manufactured in China.

CONTENTS

THE GREEK WORLD

The ancient Greeks were a very superstitious people and they worshipped many gods and goddesses. They did not have all the scientific knowledge we have today, so the Greeks relied on stories or myths about their gods to explain the world around them.

Perseus was a great Greek hero. He is famous for killing the Gorgon Medusa.

TEMPLES AND WORSHIP

The Greeks built many temples dedicated to particular gods. Priests and priestesses lived at these temples and performed special services or rituals each day. Ancient Greeks would pray at the temples and leave presents, such as olive oil, wine and animals, to encourage the gods to hear their prayers. The ancient Greeks also believed they had to ask the gods about any important events or decisions in their lives.

ORACLES AND WORSHIP

Sometimes the Greeks would visit a special priest or priestess called an oracle, in order to learn what would happen in the future. The oracle would go into a trance and then their answers would be translated by a priest. One very famous oracle was at Delphi. Here a priestess called the Pythia, would consult the god Apollo.

MYTHS AND LEGEND

Why did the Greeks tell stories? Some stories came from the need to find meaning in everyday life. Other tales were meant to make the listener think about the faults of humans. Others were invented simply to delight and entertain. The earliest Greeks told myths about the gods, but as time went on, legends developed that also described the adventures of famous heroes. For example, the legend of Jason was based on a real journey thought to have taken place around 1400 BC. However, by the time it was first written down about 1,000 years later, it had become a supernatural tale involving the gods and terrible monsters. We can see from this how oral storytelling has given us the Greek myths we know today.

This is the Acropolis in Athens. It was built in the fifth century BC and contained many sacred shrines.

Hercules was one of the most popular heroes in ancient Greece. He is shown here defeating the dragon, Ladon.

THREE GREEK MYTHS

Jason
The son of the lawful king of Iolcus. His uncle Pelias had usurped the throne.

These tales are about three different adventurers. They are typical Greek stories that explore basic themes about human nature, bravery and outwitting your enemies.

JASON AND THE ARGONAUTS

Jason is the famous hero who uses his bravery and quick thinking to find the Golden Fleece and win back the throne from his evil uncle Pelias. In order to do this, he must find a heroic crew for his ship the *Argo*, fight terrible creatures such as the dragon's tooth army and the Harpies, and find out how to survive the Clashing Rocks. Along the way he is helped by the goddess Hera, who wants to destroy Pelias, and Medea, who falls in love with him.

Medea
The daughter of Aeetes, the king of Colchis. A powerful sorceress and priestess of Hecate.

The Golden Fleece
The fleece (coat) of a ram that had once saved the boy Phrixus from sacrifice by carrying him through the air to Colchis. Aeetes then helped the boy and placed the fleece in a sacred grove guarded by a dragon.

Pelias
King of Iolcus, and Jason's uncle. He stole the throne from Jason's father.

ICARUS

The story of Icarus is still told today to warn people against carelessness, greed and disobedience. Daedalus builds two sets of wings so that he and his son can escape from their prison on Crete. However, these will only work if they do not fly too close to the sun.

Daedalus and Icarus
Daedalus was a great Athenian inventor who built the famous labyrinth for King Minos of Crete. After this, Minos kept Daedalus and his son Icarus prisoner.

Hercules
The son of Zeus and a mortal woman. His name is more commonly spelled Heracles. Hera, the wife of Zeus, was jealous of Hercules as he was the product of an affair. Zeus tried to make up for this by naming the child after Hera, hence Heracles.

Eurystheus
Hercules' cousin and king of Mycenae. Hera had tricked her husband Zeus into making him king instead of Hercules.

Ioalus
Hercules' friend and faithful servant who helped him defeat the fearsome Hydra.

THE LABOURS OF HERCULES

The Greeks loved stories of heroic deeds, and Hercules was perhaps the greatest hero of all. As a young man, Hercules had already proved himself an expert with a bow and arrow, a champion wrestler and the possessor of superhuman strength. Eventually, out of spite, Hera drove Hercules mad, and in a frenzy he killed his own wife and children. As a punishment for his crimes, he was sentenced to perform a set of tasks, also known as labours. The labours were set by his cousin, King Eurystheus.

JASON AND THE ARGONAUTS

THE GODDESS HERA WANTED REVENGE. PELIAS, KING OF IOLCUS, HAD ANGERED HER BY MURDERING HIS STEPMOTHER, SIDERO, AT THE ALTAR OF HERA'S TEMPLE. HERA HAD BEEN PATIENT. NOW SHE SAW HER CHANCE. ONE DAY, OUTSIDE THE ROYAL PALACE...

I AM JASON. I WISH TO SEE MY UNCLE, KING PELIAS.

JASON?! I THOUGHT MY NEPHEW HAD DIED AS A BABY, ALONG WITH HIS MOTHER! HMM, HE COULD MAKE TROUBLE FOR ME!

JASON! WELCOME HOME! WHERE HAVE YOU BEEN ALL THESE YEARS?

UNCLE...?

...WITH CHEIRON, THE CENTAUR. HE HAS BEEN MY TEACHER SINCE I WAS A BABY. I HAVE RETURNED TOO LATE, THOUGH. MY FATHER . . . IS DEAD.

YES, JASON. WE ALL MISS HIM.

I BECAME THE COUNTRY'S RULER AFTER YOUR FATHER DIED.

BUT UNCLE, SINCE MY FATHER WAS THE OLDER BROTHER, SHOULDN'T I NOW BE KING?

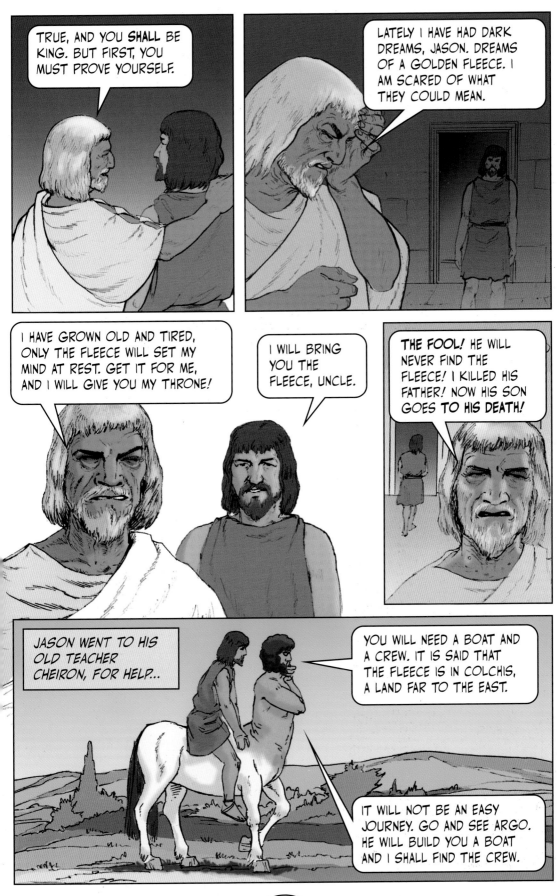

CHEIRON MADE JASON'S TASK KNOWN THROUGHOUT GREECE. MANY HEROES READY FOR AN ADVENTURE CAME TO IOLCUS. AMONG THEM WERE ORPHEUS, TELAMON, CASTOR AND POLLUX. EVEN HERCULES, THE GREATEST HERO OF ALL, JOINED THEM FOR A SHORT TIME.

MEANWHILE...

HERE SHE IS, JASON. LEAN, FAST AND SHALLOW-HULLED.

SHE'S BEAUTIFUL, ARGO.

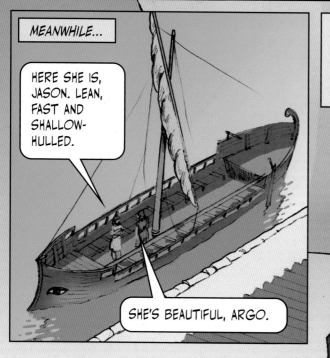

JASON NAMED THE SHIP ARGO, AFTER ITS BUILDER. ITS CREW OF HEROES WERE CALLED THE ARGONAUTS. FINALLY, THEY SET OFF ON THEIR QUEST.

TO PUNISH ME EVEN MORE, EACH DAY ZEUS SENDS HIS HARPIES TO STEAL MY FOOD. GET RID OF THEM AND I WILL TELL YOU THE WAY TO COLCHIS.

TWO OF THE ARGONAUTS, ZETES AND CALAIS, COULD FLY. WHEN THE HARPIES RETURNED...

THEY WILL NOT BE BACK, PHINEUS. NOW, HOW DO WE GET TO COLCHIS.

YOU MUST FIRST PASS THROUGH THE CLASHING ROCKS.

THE ROCKS FLOAT ON THE WATER. BUT WHEN ANYTHING TRIES TO PASS BETWEEN THEM, THE ROCKS CRASH TOGETHER, AND DESTROY IT.

WE CANNOT SAIL THROUGH THEN.

THERE IS ONE WAY...

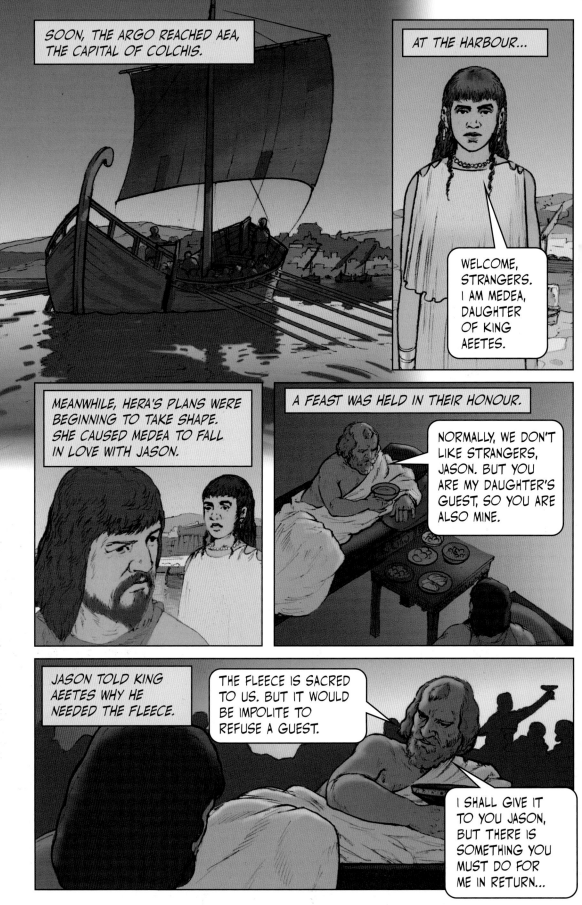

SOON, THE ARGO REACHED AEA, THE CAPITAL OF COLCHIS.

AT THE HARBOUR...

WELCOME, STRANGERS. I AM MEDEA, DAUGHTER OF KING AEETES.

MEANWHILE, HERA'S PLANS WERE BEGINNING TO TAKE SHAPE. SHE CAUSED MEDEA TO FALL IN LOVE WITH JASON.

A FEAST WAS HELD IN THEIR HONOUR.

NORMALLY, WE DON'T LIKE STRANGERS, JASON. BUT YOU ARE MY DAUGHTER'S GUEST, SO YOU ARE ALSO MINE.

JASON TOLD KING AEETES WHY HE NEEDED THE FLEECE.

THE FLEECE IS SACRED TO US. BUT IT WOULD BE IMPOLITE TO REFUSE A GUEST.

I SHALL GIVE IT TO YOU JASON, BUT THERE IS SOMETHING YOU MUST DO FOR ME IN RETURN...

14

AEETES ASKED JASON TO YOKE TWO BULLS, PLOUGH A FIELD AND SOW SOME SEEDS...

WHAT COULD BE SIMPLER, MEDEA?

THESE BULLS HAVE BRONZE HOOVES AND THEY BREATHE FIRE!

AND THE SEEDS ARE DRAGON'S TEETH. WHERE THEY ARE PLANTED, AN ARMY WILL GROW.

AS HIGH PRIESTESS OF THE TEMPLE OF HECATE, GODDESS OF MAGIC, I CAN HELP YOU..

...HERE, TAKE THIS OINTMENT. IT WILL PROTECT YOU FROM THE FIRE AND THE HOOVES.

AND THE ARMY?

THIS IS WHAT YOU MUST DO...

WITH MEDEA AND THE ARGONAUTS LOOKING ON, JASON BEGAN HIS TASK.

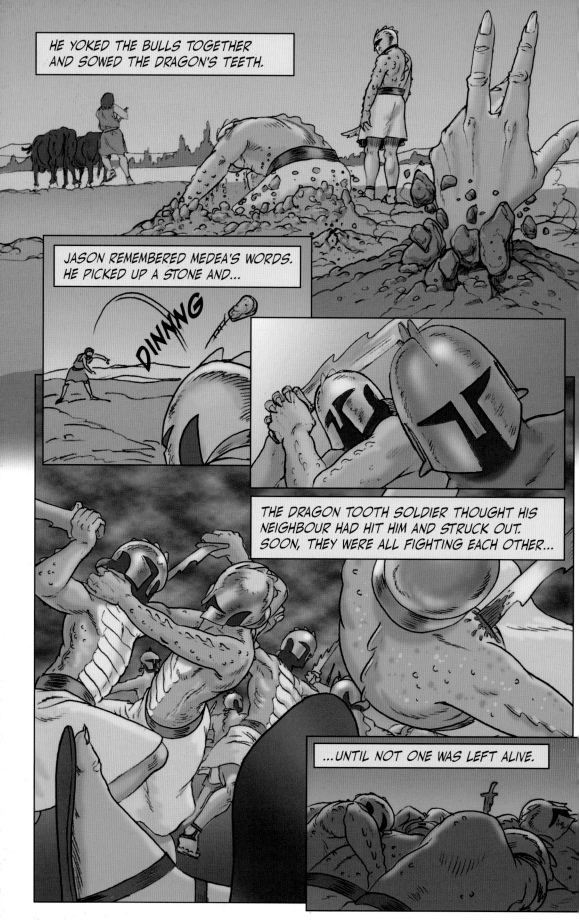

HE YOKED THE BULLS TOGETHER AND SOWED THE DRAGON'S TEETH.

JASON REMEMBERED MEDEA'S WORDS. HE PICKED UP A STONE AND...

DINNNG

THE DRAGON TOOTH SOLDIER THOUGHT HIS NEIGHBOUR HAD HIT HIM AND STRUCK OUT. SOON, THEY WERE ALL FIGHTING EACH OTHER...

...UNTIL NOT ONE WAS LEFT ALIVE.

THE ARGONAUTS FACED MANY DANGERS ON THEIR RETURN JOURNEY. ON THE ISLAND OF CRETE...

ONCE AGAIN, MEDEA'S MAGIC SAVED THEM. SHE CAUSED A ROCK TO SLIP FROM THE GIANT'S HANDS...

IT IS TALUS! THE LAST OF THE BRONZE MEN!

...AND ONTO HIS ONE WEAK SPOT.

JASON FINALLY REACHES IOLCUS.

PELIAS! HERE IS YOUR FLEECE. NOW GIVE ME THE THRONE!

JASON! HOW?

JASON! YOU HAVE THE FLEECE! YOU MUST BE TIRED. REST FIRST, YOU SHALL SOON HAVE THE CROWN.

I NEED TIME TO GET RID OF HIM!

20

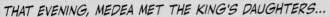
THAT EVENING, MEDEA MET THE KING'S DAUGHTERS...

KING PELIAS IS ASLEEP. YOU **MUST** DO THIS FOR THE MAGIC TO WORK. TAKE YOUR DAGGERS AND STRIKE HIM HARD, THEN POUR THE POTION OVER HIM. SOON HE WILL BECOME YOUNG AGAIN, AND YOU SHALL SEE THE FATHER YOU KNEW AS CHILDREN.

QUICKLY SISTER, THE POTION!

WHY IS NOTHING HAPPENING?!

FATHER!

THE POTION WAS **FAKE.**

WE HAVE KILLED HIM!!

PELIAS WAS DEAD, HERA GOT HER REVENGE FOR SIDERO'S MURDER AND JASON HAD BECOME KING OF IOLCUS. THE QUEST FOR THE FLEECE WAS JASON'S LAST GREAT ADVENTURE.

THE END

ICARUS

DAEDALUS, THE INVENTOR AND BUILDER, IS IN HIS WORK ROOM. HE IS BEING HELD PRISONER IN HIS HOUSE ON THE ISLAND OF CRETE BY ITS KING, MINOS. WITH HIM IS HIS SON, ICARUS.

FATHER, WHEN ARE WE GOING HOME?

SOON, ICARUS.

WHAT ARE YOU MAKING?

YOU'LL SEE.

CAN I HELP?

NO! NO, ICARUS. I CAN MANAGE.

IF YOU WANT TO HELP, WHY DON'T YOU FIND ME SOME MORE FEATHERS?

FEATHERS! IT'S ALWAYS FEATHERS THESE DAYS. WE HAVE NO FUN ANYMORE!

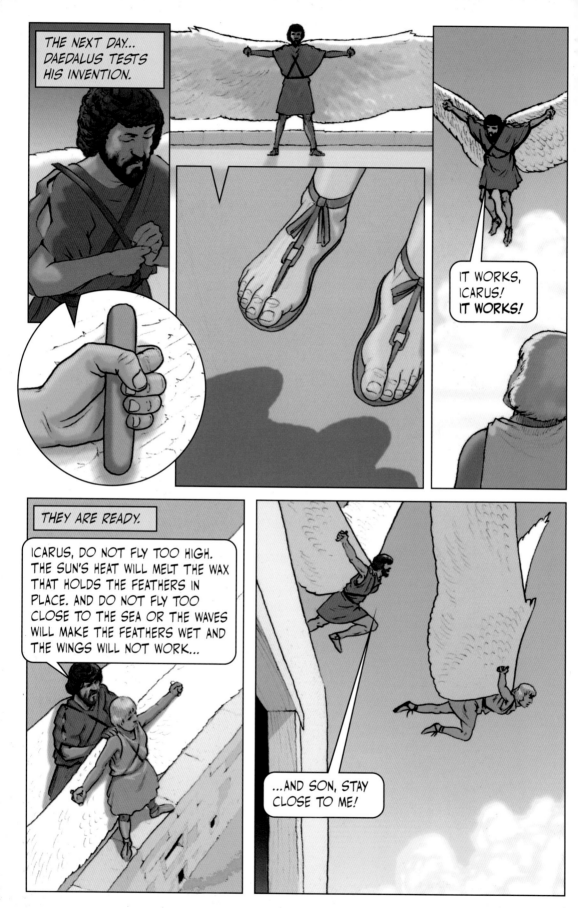

THE NEXT DAY... DAEDALUS TESTS HIS INVENTION.

IT WORKS, ICARUS! IT WORKS!

THEY ARE READY.

ICARUS, DO NOT FLY TOO HIGH. THE SUN'S HEAT WILL MELT THE WAX THAT HOLDS THE FEATHERS IN PLACE. AND DO NOT FLY TOO CLOSE TO THE SEA OR THE WAVES WILL MAKE THE FEATHERS WET AND THE WINGS WILL NOT WORK...

...AND SON, STAY CLOSE TO ME!

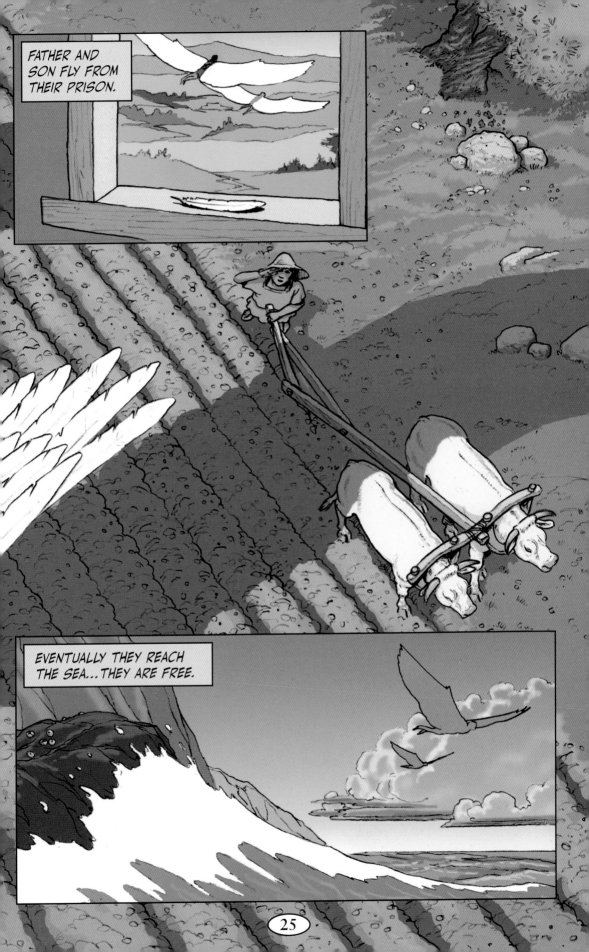

FATHER AND SON FLY FROM THEIR PRISON.

EVENTUALLY THEY REACH THE SEA...THEY ARE FREE.

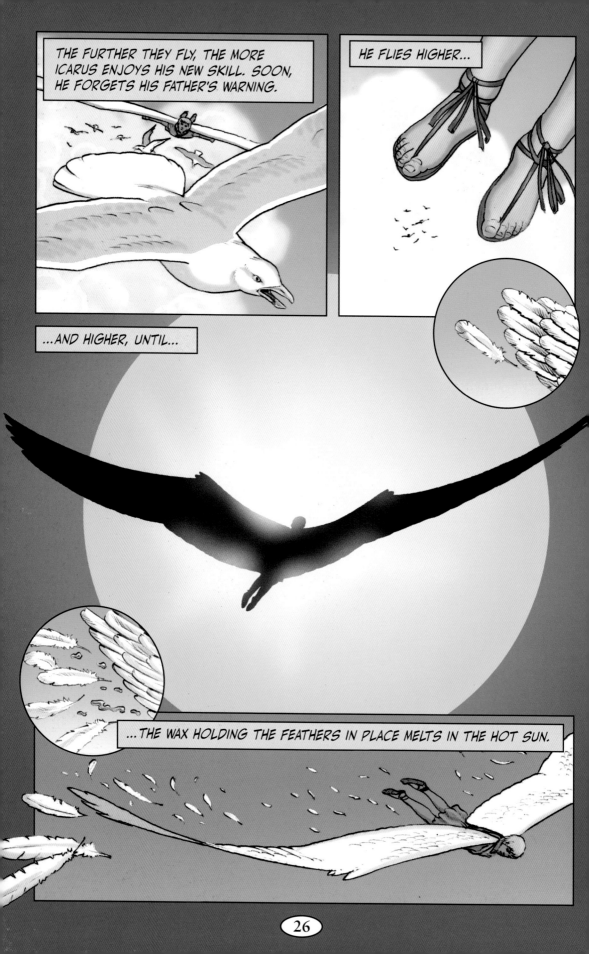

THE FURTHER THEY FLY, THE MORE ICARUS ENJOYS HIS NEW SKILL. SOON, HE FORGETS HIS FATHER'S WARNING.

HE FLIES HIGHER...

...AND HIGHER, UNTIL...

...THE WAX HOLDING THE FEATHERS IN PLACE MELTS IN THE HOT SUN.

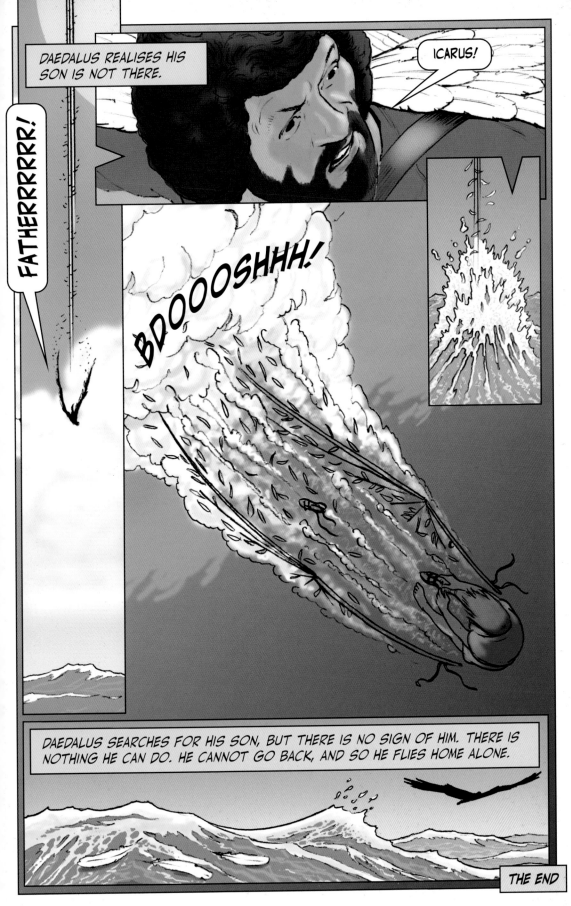

THE LABOURS OF HERCULES

HERCULES HAD FOLLOWED THE GREAT LION FOR MONTHS...

...AT LAST, THE BEAST WAS CORNERED.

ONE FINAL DASH AND...

HERCULES' CLUB AND ARROWS WERE USELESS AGAINST THE LION'S THICK MANE. HE WOULD HAVE TO KILL IT WITH HIS BARE HANDS!

THE TERROR OF THE NEMEA VALLEY, WAS DEAD – STRANGLED. HERCULES HAD COMPLETED HIS FIRST TASK.

WHY HAD HERCULES KILLED THE LION? IN A FIT OF MADNESS BROUGHT ON BY HIS STEPMOTHER, THE GODDESS HERA, HERCULES HAD KILLED HIS OWN WIFE AND CHILDREN. TO PUNISH HIM, THE GODS HAD FORCED HERCULES TO SERVE HIS COUSIN, EURYSTHEUS, THE KING OF MYCENAE, AND PERFORM TEN HEROIC TASKS, OR LABOURS. HERCULES NOW RETURNED TO MYCENAE TO BE GIVEN HIS SECOND TASK.

AT THE COURT OF KING EURYSTHEUS...

WAKE UP, SIRE.

WHAA?

ARGH! THE NEMEAN LION HAS COME TO EAT ME!

THE NEMEAN LION IS DEAD...

...HERE IS ITS SKIN.

ER, WELL DONE HERCULES. YOU KEEP IT. SOMEONE WILL GIVE YOU YOUR NEXT TASK. I HAVE TO GO.

THE MAN'S A MENACE! IN THE FUTURE, DON'T LET HIM NEAR THE PALACE! WHO KNOWS WHAT DAMAGE HE COULD DO?

I NEVER LIKED HIM WHEN WE WERE CHILDREN! WHY COULDN'T HERCULES AND THE LION HAVE KILLED EACH OTHER!

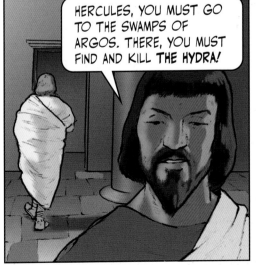

HERCULES, YOU MUST GO TO THE SWAMPS OF ARGOS. THERE, YOU MUST FIND AND KILL THE HYDRA!

FOR EVERY HEAD THAT HERCULES CUT OFF, TWO GREW IN ITS PLACE.

DO YOU NEED SOME HELP, HERCULES?

IOLAUS! QUICK! LIGHT A FIRE!

IOLAUS USED A FLAMING TORCH TO BURN THE HEADLESS STUMPS BEFORE MORE HEADS COULD GROW BACK.

TSSSZZZZZ!!!

SOON, ONLY ONE HEAD WAS LEFT – THE LARGEST.

HERCULES BURIED THE HUGE HEAD.

JUST TO MAKE SURE IT STAYS DEAD!

BACK IN MYCENAE...

WHERE'S EURYSTHEUS?

HE'S OVER THERE.

AFTER YOUR LAST VISIT, EURYSTHEUS HAD THAT LARGE BRONZE POT MADE AND BURIED. HE SAYS HE FEELS SAFER IN IT WHEN YOU'RE AROUND, HERCULES.

GET ON WITH IT!

HERE IS THE THIRD TASK HERCULES...

EURYSTHEUS WANTED THE HIND OF CERYNEIA. THE DEER HAD GOLDEN HORNS AND BRONZE HOOVES. IT WAS THE GODDESS DIANA'S PET. HERCULES CHASED THE DEER FOR A YEAR UNTIL HE FINALLY MANAGED TO WOUND AND CATCH IT.

BUT HE WAS STOPPED BY DIANA. WHEN SHE SAW HER WOUNDED PET, SHE BECAME ANGRY. HERCULES EXPLAINED ABOUT THE TASKS AND DIANA FORGAVE HIM. SHE HEALED THE DEER'S WOUND AND LET HERCULES TAKE HER PET TO MYCENAE.

FOR HIS NEXT TASK, HERCULES HAD TO GO TO MOUNT ERYMANTHUS WHERE A GIANT BOAR HAD BEEN TERRORISING THE COUNTRYSIDE. HERCULES HAD TO BRING IT BACK TO MYCENAE - ALIVE!

ON THE WAY TO MYCENAE...

SQUEEEEEEEAL!

WILL YOU JUST STOP WRIGGLING!

32

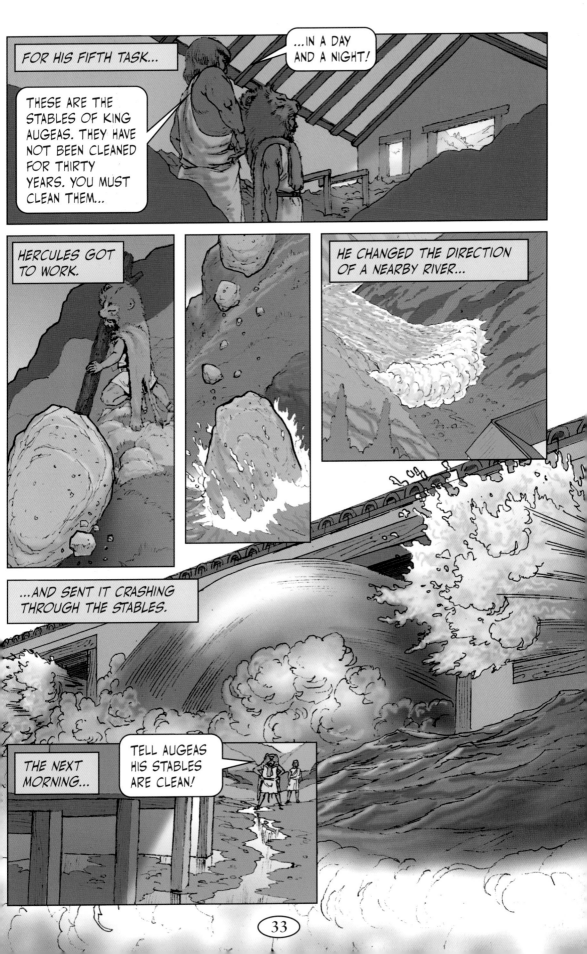

FOR HIS SIXTH TASK, HERCULES HAD TO DRIVE AWAY A HUGE FLOCK OF BIRDS FROM THE TOWN OF STYMPHALOS.

TO HELP HIM, THE GODDESS ATHENA HAD GIVEN HERCULES A PAIR OF MAGIC CYMBALS.

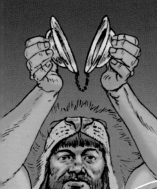

THE NOISE FROM THE CYMBALS . . .

KERLANNGGG!!

SCARED THE BIRDS INTO THE AIR WHERE THEY WERE SHOT.

THE SIXTH TASK WAS OVER.

HERCULES EASILY CAUGHT THE CRETAN BULL TO COMPLETE HIS SEVENTH TASK...

...AND TOOK THE FLESH-EATING HORSES OF DIOMEDES BACK TO EURYSTHEUS FOR HIS EIGHTH TASK.

FOR HIS NINTH TASK, HERCULES HAD TO BRING BACK THE GIRDLE OF HIPPOLYTA, QUEEN OF THE AMAZONS. HIPPOLYTA AGREED TO GIVE HER GIRDLE TO HERCULES, BUT AS HERCULES AND HIPPOLYTA WERE SAYING GOODBYE, HERA, IN DISGUISE, SPREAD RUMOURS THAT THEIR QUEEN WAS BEING KIDNAPPED. THE AMAZONS ATTACKED HERCULES, AND HIPPOLYTA WAS KILLED.

IN MYCENAE...

I THOUGHT IT WOULD BE FUN HAVING HERCULES AS A SLAVE FOR A WHILE. BUT HE'S CAUSED ME NOTHING BUT TROUBLE!

THE COUNTRYSIDE IS NOW FULL OF ALL THE DANGEROUS BEASTS HE'S BROUGHT BACK.

AND THE PEOPLE THINK HE'S A HERO. WHERE IS HERCULES NOW?

BRINGING YOU THE RED CATTLE OF GERYON, SIRE.

LET'S HOPE HE TAKES HIS TIME.

LADIES AND GENTLEMEN! LOOK! ALL THE TASKS OF HERCULES DECORATE THESE POTS AND VASES...

36

THREE GOLDEN APPLES BELONGING TO HERA WERE KEPT IN THE GARDEN OF THE HESPERIDES. THEY WERE GUARDED BY A DRAGON AND THREE MAIDENS CALLED THE HESPERIDES.

HERCULES DID NOT KNOW WHERE THE GARDEN WAS, OR HOW TO GET THE APPLES, BUT EURYSTHEUS WANTED THEM. HERCULES WENT TO SEE ATLAS, THE HESPERIDES' FATHER...

ATLAS WAS A TITAN, ONE OF THE FIRST GODS. FOR MAKING WAR AGAINST ZEUS, HE HAD BEEN CONDEMNED TO HOLD UP THE HEAVENS FOREVER.

HERCULES EXPLAINED TO ATLAS WHY HE WAS THERE.

AS THEIR FATHER, ONLY YOU CAN PERSUADE THE HESPERIDES TO LEND ME THE GOLDEN APPLES, ATLAS.

HOW CAN I GET THE APPLES, HERCULES? WHAT WOULD HAPPEN TO THE HEAVENS IF I LEFT?

LET ME HOLD THE SKY WHILE YOU ARE GONE.

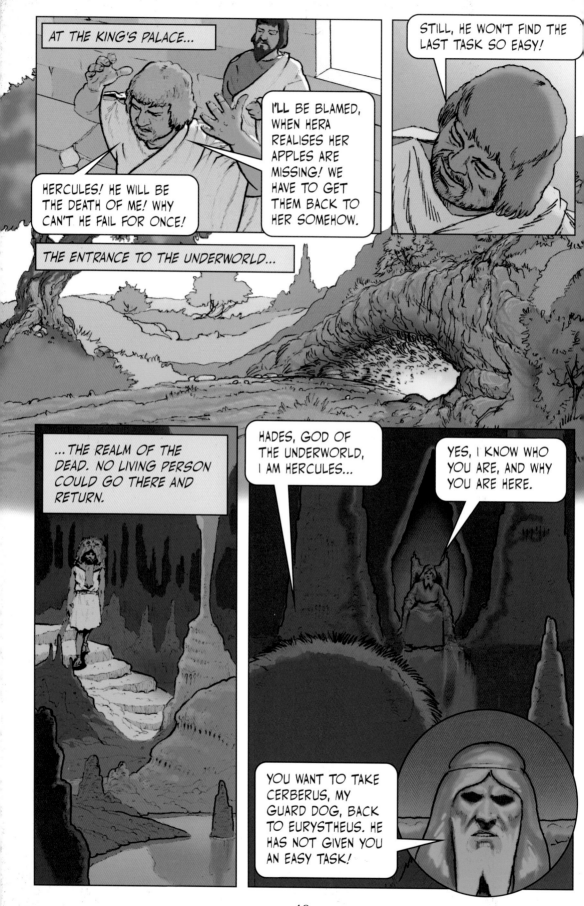

IF YOU FAIL, HERCULES, YOU WILL HAVE TO STAY HERE FOREVER.

I WILL LET YOU BORROW CERBERUS ON ONE CONDITION...

...YOU MAY NOT USE A WEAPON OF ANY KIND AGAINST HIM.

SO, HERCULES, IF YOU WANT MY PET...

...TAME HIM!

ONCE IN THE DAYLIGHT...

...CERBERUS WAS BEATEN.

HERCULES TOOK CERBERUS BACK TO MYCENAE.

I WONDER WHAT EURYSTHEUS WILL SAY WHEN HE SEES YOU!

HERE BOY, FETCH!

ONCE EURYSTHEUS HAD SEEN HIM, HERCULES LET CERBERUS RETURN TO HADES. THE LAST TASK HAD BEEN COMPLETED. HERCULES HAD PAID FOR THE MURDER OF HIS FAMILY. HE HAD WON THE RIGHT TO LIVE WITH THE GODS AFTER HIS DEATH. ...AND AS FOR EURYSTHEUS...

...ARE YOU **SURE** THEY'VE GONE?

THE END

43

MORE MYTHICAL CHARACTERS

Originating from many different myths and legends, Greek mythology is a treasure chest of colourful, larger-than-life characters. Here is a small selection of heroes, kings, monsters and gods.

ACHILLES — A Greek hero who fought at Troy. Achilles was impossible to harm, except for his heel. He killed Hector but was in turn killed by Paris.

APHRODITE — The goddess of love and beauty. She was born fully formed from the sea foam at Paphos in Cyprus.

APOLLO — The god of music and poetry. He was the son of Zeus and was associated with the sun. He was the twin brother of Artemis.

ARES — The son of Zeus and Hera, and the god of war.

ARTEMIS — The goddess of the moon and the twin sister of Apollo.

ATHENA — The goddess of war and wisdom. She was not born but emerged, fully-formed, from the head of Zeus. Athens was named in her honour.

CENTAURS — A race of creatures that had the body of a human and the legs of a horse.

HADES — God of the dead and ruler of the underworld.

HERA — The wife of Zeus, and the goddess of women and marriage. She protected Jason, but was the enemy of Hercules.

MEDUSA — The name of the most terrible Gorgon sister. She was mortal, but it was nearly impossible to kill her because one look at her would turn anyone to stone. She was killed by Perseus with Athena's help.

MINOTAUR — A creature that was half-man and half-bull. He was the son of Pasophae (wife of Minos) and a bull from the sea. Minos kept him in the labyrinth made by Daedalus, and fed him Athenian youths. Eventually, he was killed by Theseus.

PANDORA — Pandora, the first woman, was made by Hephaestus. Zeus gave her a box, which she was told never to open. She became curious and opened it and so released evil into the world.

PEGASUS — A winged horse that sprang from the blood of Medusa, after she was killed by Perseus.

PERSEUS — The son of Zeus and Danae, he and his mother were put in a chest and thrown into the sea by Acrisius, Danae's father. Perseus grew up to defeat Medusa the Gorgon.

POSEIDON — The god of water and the sea. Poseidon was the brother of Zeus and Hades and is usually shown with a trident in his hand.

THESEUS — The king and national hero of Athens, Theseus is most famous for conquering the Amazons and killing the Minotaur.

THE TITANS — The twelve children of Uranus and Gaea. They were the older generation of gods. Zeus and Hera were the children of Cronus, one of the Titans. When Zeus and the Olympians took power, the Titans made war on them and the Titans were defeated.

ZEUS — The god of the sky and the supreme Olympian, Zeus was married to Hera. He fathered many children, including both gods, goddesses, and mortals such as Perseus.

GLOSSARY

Amazon A member of a nation of female warriors from Scythia.

Athenian A person who lives in or comes from Athens, in Greece.

betrayed To have turned against someone.

capital The main city in a country and the seat of its government.

condemned To be blamed or punished for a crime.

conquer To defeat another land using weapons.

constellation A group of stars.

girdle A belt that goes around the wearer's waist.

grove A small group of trees.

Harpies Vicious winged monsters with the head and body of a woman, and the tail, wings and claws of a bird.

hind A female deer.

Hydra A giant snake with many heads.

inventor Somebody who first designs or makes an item.

labours Tasks such as those performed by Hercules.

labyrinth A structure with many passages that is hard to get out of.

maiden A young woman.

ointment A liquid that is applied to the skin to heal or protect it.

oracle Someone who is considered to be very wise and can predict the future. An oracle can also talk with the gods.

potion A magic liquid that is either medicinal or poisonous.

prophecy A prediction of the future.

revenge To get even with someone who has hurt you by doing something unpleasant to them.

sacred When something is religious or holy.

seer A prophet who sees visions of the future.

sow To plant seeds in the ground.

superstitious A fear of the unknown, or of religion or magic.

terrorise To fill someone with fear or dread.

trident A spear or sceptre with three prongs like a fork.

tyrant A king or leader who rules through fear and cruelty.

underworld The world of the dead, which is underneath the world of the living.

usurp To take control of a throne or position illegally.

worship Ceremonies and prayers dedicated to a god or gods.

yoke A wooden bar used to attach a plough to cows or oxen.

FOR MORE INFORMATION

ORGANISATIONS

The British Museum
Great Russell Street
London, WC1B 3DG
www.thebritishmuseum.ac.uk

Shefton Museum of Greek Art and Archaeology
University of Newcastle, Armstrong Building
Newcastle upon Tyne, NE1 7RU
www.ncl.ac.uk/shefton-museum

FOR FURTHER READING
If you liked this book, you might also want to try:

Inside Ancient Athens
by Fiona Macdonald, Book House 2005

The Wooden Horse of Troy
by John Malam, Book House 2004

The Adventures of Perseus
by Peter Hepplewhite, Book House 2004

The Twelve Labours of Heracles
by James Ford, Book House 2004

Graphic Myths: Roman
by David West, Book House 2006

INDEX

Web Sites

Due to the changing nature of Internet links, the Salariya Book Company has developed an online list of Web sites related to the subject of this book. This site is updated regularly. Please use this link to access the list:

http://www.book-house.co.uk/gmyth/greek